PRINCE
OF PEACE

SECOND COMING

PRINCE OF PEACE

SECOND COMING

JOHN RUONAVAARA

ISBN 979-8-89175-193-4 (sc)

Prince of Peace and The Second Coming

R
U
O
JOHNELS
A
V
A
A
R
A

Wonderful, Counsellor, The mighty God, The everlasting Father, The Prince of Peace.

Prince of Peace will be a Second Coming Revelation and a testimony to the in-depth measure of the awakened new coming to the end of the world.

Savior like a Shepherd lead us, this is my heart's desire and prayer, that it's Thy will be done.

Deliverance to the son of man.

Revelation 3:12 Him that overcomes will I make a pillar in the temple of my God, and he shall go no more out: and I will write upon him the name of my God, and the name of the city of my God, which is new Jerusalem, which cometh down out of heaven from my God: and I will write upon him my new name.

This book will open new life, new light, and provide promising tokens of inspiration and to the spiritual bond of charity related to the Second Coming.

We are nearing the end of the world or the end of time. The world's largest event that also is written in Holy Scripture about The Son of Man coming into Power, The New Jerusalem, City of a Living God, all the many promises in the Bible about Jesus Coming with Power and Glory.

Revelation 14:2 And I heard a voice from heaven, as the voice of many waters, and as the voice of a great thunder: and I heard the voice of harpers harping with their harps:

This book Prince of Peace will illustrate revelation or inspiration onto the coming of a new world and to the honor of God.

2 Thessalonians 2:15 Therefore, brethren, stand fast, and hold the traditions which ye have been taught, whether by word, or our epistle.

My name is John and through interpretation Spiritual Jesus.

I am a Spiritual Jew, Jesus is in my heart through Faith I am not of the Jewish descent, but I have Living Faith in Christianity and Jesus was born through the conception of the Holy Ghost in my heart.

I've had broken and contrite hearts and sorrow after the mind of God and his righteousness, also into the breaking of bread. This is found in forgiveness and to the remission of sin. I have a testimony over my soul I am a traveling, Christian.

(I observe all things), with the eyes of Faith, communion of body and blood everlasting. You can see in the Holy Scripture how Jesus loved John the most, John bestowed Love. This book is also related to the same brotherly Love that John portrayed to Jesus.

Being "chosen" by God is not about being better than others, but about being willing to respond to God's will.

Faith, Hope, and Charity but the Greatest of these is Charity. Without love and the redeeming effort of our Lord and Savior who had suffered and died on the cross we would be left empty of his Redeeming grace.

I have no other refuge than that you would pray on my behalf with thy will be done. I have had a heavy and difficult journey, so if you're reading this book, please pray.

In this book I have submitted information that probably exceeds most people's expectations, but this truly is my soul traveling experience.

1 Corinthians 13:2 And though I have the gift of prophecy, and understand all mysteries, and all knowledge; and though I have all faith, so that I could remove mountains, and have not charity, I am nothing.

Dear brothers and sisters of faith, join our hearts in prayer that God would lead the journey and open the door for promises that this would be an encouragement for all of us.

We are all the family of creation. God created man after his image this my friend yes this my friend is true. We all grieve or ponder the emptiness that something is missing. Even though we have made endeavors in our life and we are successful at what we do we've all heard or thought about the end of the world and Bible prophecy which also supports the

Second Coming. The grievances of the end of the world do not play exempt on anyone; we all feel that something uncertain that hasn't happened yet is pending. Yes, this is true we are children in a flock even though we have our independencies even though we have our differences even though we have our struggles or suffering we are children of the same (hope) that my children would have a bright future or that someday God will lift this Vale.

I grew up in the old apostolic Lutheran Church in the Hancock area. The old apostolic Lutheran Church follows the Holy Scripture as the closest, and you can see it in their example. I was baptized and confirmed, and I also had a distant marriage. I have endured a mental health duration and went through many hospital visits. I am on medication. I do not have any more symptoms or side effects. This is what medicine can do, and I'm very grateful for it. I do have some anxiety sometimes.

It is written in the Holy Scripture that the Son of Man must suffer many things and because of that I've had to walk alone.

To the individuals or people that are struggling with mental illness, (I love you).

Those of you who may be reading this book and do not identify themselves as a Christian I have the compassion of Love towards you as well with an extended salutations and the highest greeting of (God's Peace).

The spirituality might have a Christian conduct but it's for the love of humanity across the world, my hand is not shortened simply because you are not a following Christian no, we are children in the flock of spirituality.

When the voice of the trumpet begins to sound, warm winds of Awakening will begin to affect each and every one of us, the end of the world is depicted as a dark, no, we want to hope of all things, my dear brother and sister we live in a dark time now it's as in the days of Noah even though people are giving in to marriage and having feasts, the darkness or uncertainty can be felt by millions right now.

The Second Coming and Warm Winds of Awakening will affect each and every one of us according to our proportion of faith. We are traveling to a reconciliation with God. Surely you will see the son of man Jesus John his true name with the eyes of bloody clouds (singing) in the land of the New Jerusalem.

I have heard of living water flowing within Zion's walls.

As of the first fruits Jesus he also had the God-head mind. This is what it means about the Second Coming; I am that I am.

We will be known also as he shall be known, can you imagine whether you're living across the world or even in your local hometown like me Hancock Houghton people will feel this Spiritual warmth, it could be in the middle of winter and it would feel like springtime, it's God in an awesome wonder. The human race will feel like a family something that has never been manifested, this is powerful oh is this powerful, people will be in some ways ecstatic and in other ways compassionate to each other. Saluting each other with God's Peace, doesn't it say oh come let us adore thee, I am not my own, but chosen of God through revelation, we all have different spiritual interpretations that also have a mutual relationship based on our experience.

(Mystery of the Gospel)

"Let us pray in Faith that the bloody clouds would rain into the open and moved fields of the heart so that the Son of Righteousness could shine with the Power of His Resurrection."

Our Elders and Mothering congregation in Swedish Lapland that has taken so much good care of Christianity here in America and Europe have written these words about the bloody clouds it has to do with the reconciliation and the contrite heart of forgiveness.

Jesus' first miracles, he turned water into wine. Its mutual spiritual pattern can be interpreted according to these Spiritual warm winds of Awakening to that reference of spiritual wine, which is also referred to as turning (coldness into fervency). Raining tears of pain into tears of joy for the reconciliation of the forgiveness of sins. Tears of joy are the blossoming fruits of righteousness. Through this reconciliation, we would have life, and a free conscience, exchanging sin for grace. When the sermon of repentance is being preached by the light and power of the Holy Ghost, the word of God and the spoken word of God, this is where we find ourselves and that we would see ourselves as we truly are. That God is the revealer of all great things if he can start the good work in you, he can also finish the good work, Alpha and Omega he is the beginning and end.

Will the son of man find faith on Earth? This is written in the Holy Scripture I had to travel holding Jesus name, with a silent seal for many, many years, how do you talk about spiritual matters without giving the indication that supports grandiosity or being puffed up, it is never been my indication to represent something that I did not solely believe was prophesied in thy behalf. John and Jesus share something in common it's our nickname, (disturber of the people) I went years of having the courage to express spiritual zeal and out of all the times I just got so upset that it showed symptoms of a mental illness so I ended up hospitalized. I've always had an overpowering conviction. I relate to this as a unquenchable spirit or also considered an unquenchable fire. I was hospitalized many times for about a week each time. I knew something was different in my life. I was just not able to identify what to do with this revelation and these revelations happened a lot through my life. I lost many jobs I lost marriage I lost relationships. I had an inward conviction and I quietly believed I was Jesus. I couldn't say it without attracting controversy. I was always a deeper thinker in my philosophy and spirituality. I felt like I was being victimized over and over because I had all the symptoms of a mental health condition of which I do, but, it was also intertwined to spiritual experience. So this book is about my spiritual interpretation.

Divine God in a Spiritual realm. I am a witness and a sacrifice to the testimonies of Holy Scripture and with love I'm just a child.

When we pray at night we pray to Most High the eternal God Most High.

This is the second manifestation of a sacrifice. Sacrificing for the Love of mankind.

That I would lay down my life to help and inspire mankind that's a sacrifice of Love, Love is the most Greatest attribute of perfection.

(Coming unto the fullness of Christ)

1 Corinthians 13:10 But when that which is perfect is come, then that which is in part shall be done away.

Spiritual Lord and Savior, Its this little child, that wins our heart to believe. A precious redeeming soul, yes we will find this child in our hearts. As Servant Lord and Savior proclaiming the sermon of Repentance. That's where the grace that is given unto us is shed with the open arms and the fountains of grace. That it's a free access to The fountains of cleansing and to the blood of sprinkling by his Mercy and through his Love.

The only reason this child has endured so much is because of Love. I certainly do have a Great Love for humanity.

It is written, that Jesus set a little child in the midst of them, did he not proclaim and who is this little child it says for whosoever shall become as a little child the same is likened in the kingdom of heaven. It's conceived through childlike believing overcoming adversity by accepting the will of God from the love of the heart. Submissive to the will of God, that's how you truly deny yourself "it's never been my will but it's always been thy will"

1 Corinthians 13:11 When I was a child, I spake as a child, I understood as a child, I thought as a child: but when I became a man, I put away childish things. That's what that means that we would be no longer children tossed to and fro what does that look like? It looks like a hypocritical unbeliever if you're hypocritical you are looking into the glass darkly we want to see ourselves face to face that you do not straight away forget like a child you are responsible man that's why it says I put away childish things. You neglect and deny the power of your own faith. If you support vulnerability to do things in your life that are not healthy and that causes offense or wound on the conscience then you have opened the door of permissibility. We want to have a firm foundation and hold fast as a Stewart in Christianity.

"This world has never felt spiritual warmth"

Jesus is king of creation tidings for the young and old. He is Lord of the Heavenly Pilot. He is the barer of burdens Lord of lords. He is that child countenance of the son of God.

He says behold I come quickly, what this means is that the cognition of human chemistry is so well equipped that in the speaking and spoken word of God at the Deliverance is magnified not only in his heart but to the dear children and listening witness of the elect fold of God watching.

How can I hold Jesus in my heart this is so precious each and everyone I love you so much sometimes there's so much spam in life that you can't make it through until you find the right door maybe this book is the right door or the right opportunity to really get out that I'm not just a plastic bag blowing away in the wind. Jesus said my God my God why has thou forsaken me, I think we've all felt this way at certain times in our life.

Must Jesus bear the cross alone and all the world go free, no there's a cross for everyone and there is one me.

Where is the foot of the cross when we have turmoil or differences in our opinions and maybe lose our temper where do we turn to, in order to find the foot of the cross. Oh yes dear father and mother oh yes dear child the foot of the cross is at the neck of one another, embracing each other asking for forgiveness, the testimony of the forgiveness of sins is found with a humble and contrite heart, testifying.

"believe all sins forgiven in Jesus Holy Name and precious reconciling blood, never remember again, drowned in the depths of the sea".

These are the encouraging words we can tell one another and proclaim the forgiveness of sins. Yes we certainly want to pray for one another and as much as God gives me strength.

When we have a reconciliation we have a testimony, and it's written in our hearts by Faith. I have heard that one drop of Jesus blood is so powerful it can cleanse seven worlds and it is shed for you and for many.

Through the Trumpet Voice of many waters we will hear the rolling thunder. Oh come ye all faithful joyful and triumphant. When I was a child I become very "distressed" because of what I have done and how I treated my mom my dad scolded me before I was going to sleep and says you cannot do that you hurt your mom and you should not go to sleep like that, you need to say sorry to Mom and because of that I become deeply sorrowful and wounded, I went to my mom and dad's bedside and asked for forgiveness and said sorry to Mom and Dad that was my earliest experience of forgiveness and Christianity in the home. God is truly the lover of our soul that's why it's called a children's Kingdom.

(There many shall come from the East and the West to sit at the feast of Salvation) as lightning cometh out of the East and into the West so shall the Son of man be. From the rising to the resurrection of the Sun as the Holy Scripture so promises that a new day will dawn that our hearts will be set at liberty where are soul is pure and clean.

I do most certainly believe that we can work with DNA and come up with The fountains of youth or relation to stem cell using our God-given DNA from the birth of Adam so that we would become perfect in our ways no more down syndrome no more illnesses, God will bless this journey doesn't it say in the Holy Scripture, I am with you even unto the end of the world.

Behold a great cloud of witnesses and an innumerable company of angels.

If God is on our side who can be against us.

What's been done of sin, the law of God's eternal righteousness must prick the heart by Faith that's where Jesus will enter and then the kingdom of heaven can be revealed that's a very small door. By choosing the Love from the heart each and everyone of us that's how we find ourselves and that's how we carry the Lord Jesus in our heart and when that's done mankind will hold the chapter of love in their bosom.

John 1:26-27 John answered them, saying, I baptize with water: but there standeth one among you, whom ye know not;

He It is, who coming after me is preferred before me, whose shoe's latchet I am not worthy to unloose.

Spiritual Jesus and the Second Coming, I am that I am. Our God is a consuming fire.

Do you believe Jesus is the door before you, yes, I certainly feel the same way he is always been the door before me even taking on the name of Spiritual Jesus. It won't be long until these trumpets begin to sound.

In My Father's House there are many mansions, yes this is true, I do have complete conceptual designs of this Father's House and the many Mansions High. This will be built at a chosen location and be used for Christmas and St John's time and possibly spring and fall meeting's, heavenly meetings where more people can gather. The Lord's House is small but the Father's house is beautiful and much, much bigger. I have a design for this that has a rosewood altar absolutely beautiful. It also has a library with glass doors people can come to the Father's house whenever especially around Christmas time. The church benches are made out of oak and maple and they have a red cushion on the seat. In between each Mansion as it goes up there are two pillars dividing the next mansion. The warm lighting in the sanctuary makes the place glow with comfort. The lighting in the mansions are hanging glass chandeliers that are closer to the ceiling. Similar to the Stockholm contemporary lights or Ikea and then 3 ft by 1 ft hanging lamps that are circular and glow at different brightness. The windows have optional tinting. Also there's a pretty big breezeway or entryway that connects to the kitchen in the back a two-story kitchen with escalators. Like I have mentioned before I'm just a child but yes I have Big dreams I am a man child I even feel sheepish saying it.

Daniel 8:24-25 And his power shall be mighty, but not by his own power: and he shall destroy wonderfully, and shall prosper, and practise, and shall destroy the mighty and the holy people.

And through his policy also he shall cause craft to prosper in his hand; and he shall magnify himself in his heart, and by peace shall destroy many: he shall also stand up against the Prince of princes; but he shall be broken without hand.

The humble side of God it says broken without hand that's God and his ultimate humility oh is this precious.

If you believe that you have a strong God, you will receive him as a strong God. We have trials that go through a duration in our lives but that's the power of prayer, that we would never underestimate the power of prayer.

I have a Goal of becoming President of the United States of America I don't know when but I would like to run for 2028 I'll be willing to take over presidency at any time it doesn't have to be on 2028. I willingly respect due process but if help is needed I can help. What I do as a President has never been seen and has never been practiced I am unique I have a peculiar sense of philosophy and childlike curiosity with a intelligent courageousness towards life. One of the first things I would work on as president would be building immigration hubs on the border these massive hubs are designed to educate and do job training. They're designed like stadiums so that the kids and parents can be in a place of refuge until they're able to find a place in the states or if it worked in other countries as well getting people established so they can also go into independence with their own home. My idea is to provide these hubs with raw product for example fabric and food and then they can have patterns and make clothes for their people in that hub and also for the food as well give them recipes similar to what you see and food courts inside malls and restaurants and other home cooked meals. In the evening time the kids and parents can watch cartoons or educational videos and also have sleeping arrangements inside the stadium and bedrooms on the inside of a stadium exterior.

Also, I have a brand new institution called The Center of Reconstitute, also known by as Team-6. Team 6 is structured as a goal oriented facility. The software program that is connected to an iPad helps people achieve their goals by starting their day coming up with a goal for the day and then trying to achieve that throughout the day. If you were able to meet your goal you are able to give a five-star rating and what worked best for you in achieving that goal. Each person has their independent or individual goal and then the team between six members works on what they want to do as a group that week. It can be anything from a fishing adventure or shopping experience of the many different things that can be chosen from especially including helping elderly make it to their appointment and have a lunch. The idea of this team six is so people can have a refuge with sleeping arrangements that look like huts inside a (Ikea) style Warehouse and feel like they're part of something rather than independently suffering at home. I'm sure there's other ways to improve this institution from input from other people as well but in the morning there's a continental breakfast and a massive office like interior.

Part of this Center of reconstitute supports prison reform as well for both female and male. We need to have ways or find ways for people to achieve responsibility be able to obtain personal accountability and measure their growth by their goals that they have reached.

One of the other areas of interest that I have been working on for a while is a software program related to the seven golden candlesticks. The Holy Scripture writes of the seven golden candlesticks. Which are identities related to (core inventor) product development or new ideas. This is many times bigger than Amazon. I referred to it as a brand new global stock market it has the ability to capture products related to the product developer and if it meets all seven identities on the software program that product is the main product on the market. You are now the Creator of that product, that way we don't have multiple products of the same kind. It would turn the entire world into a global competition so for example, if you know how to make a better hammer you can achieve this goal and become the origin or inventor of that product so this can always be improved upon that's why they're called seven golden candlesticks. It's like gold tried in fire and continues to purify. This global stock market can also bring the world to One World Government One New World Order. Also, bringing appropriate measures for Moral Conduct, so in all things we can market the train of thought and what works well in some experiences.

I will also bring you the kingdom of heaven. I have a cocoon project that I refer to as the kingdom of heaven it has to do with advanced technologies related to augmentation. The kingdom of heaven is like stepping into a massive peach shell and when you're inside sitting down or laying down you can experience the highest form of quality to natural habitations that this world has never seen, a gentle breeze and the scent and three dimensional augmentation. Augmentation is a massive undertaking to the new world to come it is the biggest leap of mankind to the glory of God and also to the honor of God that we would not pervert this with things related to inordinate affection or things that are perverted and offensive. That we do not want sinful behavior that develops spiritual harm. There are other areas in this Kingdom of heaven augmentation or virtual reality that I can stress on as well. Another part of augmentation our kids studying in cubicles that are all virtual reality so you can create an environment and meet your classmates face to face or in a circle once the kid goes in for class everything's turned on and that child watches the teacher in the middle.

Another big development in the civil engineering department would be Shepherd blue rail. Shepherd blue rail is a pipeline system that goes in the sky about 40 ft or 50 ft and can cross valleys without building big Bridges it's a three pipe system. This system glows at night time bright blue and it helps for traffic if you wanted to travel to which would be a 8 hour distance in the past would come down to an hour half hour to travel. These Bots are just like a car interior and there's also ones that can be done as a train as well and can also deliver packages. The system is independent for transportation communication and does not need GPS coordinates for it has its own navigational built-in system. Shepherd blue rail can travel across oceans with a telescoping balance flotation to help guide but also smooth ride transportations.

I have also touched base on some new possibilities of having biological calendars that way if you're planning a trip somewhere everyone that's on the helping end of that organizes your trip with you in order to have the best of your experience on vacation or if you're somewhere for a doctor's appointment the people that are on the working end of that spectrum or calendar help out, it would give humanity a brand new start. How would you like to be an elderly person and have all these helping hands to make your doctor visit awesome that's the benefits of biological calendars everyone pitches in we are a human race now with dignity wow.

I love you guys so much maybe it's hard to put on paper to really appreciate but I work so hard but I also just want to take this moment and extend my love for you. Wow I love you, the reason why I'm so passionate at the moment is because I know you will get this I know this is something that is favored some of the stuff that I would be presenting as a President of the United States of America the best working platform for this Deliverance.

That's the heart's desire, is that, we would be able to make the uncommon common so that we are one minded with our universal intent. Related to human decency and Moral law. Moral value and Moral conduct, so it will always be, We the people For the people By the people. We will be traveling in complete perfection. God is not the author of confusion. We are traveling to an eternity of awesomeness this is so so precious.

God truly is love but he also has his righteousness those two are hand in hand and neither one of them can overcome the other Truth and Love.

In our travel sometimes just by simply changing your behavior is not enough it needs a reconciliation sometimes especially if someone is really wounded The mystery of the Gospel is found through forgiveness. I understand it's sometimes better to change your attitude this works as well on restoring friendships. Although we want to be mindful of repentance.

We must believe in the forgiveness of sins so that God would open his grace and exchange sin for grace. This is so precious and it relates to how we become soul travelers on the road to eternity and in so doing that our soul would be purified. Oh dear repentant soul yes I encourage you as well that the door of grace would not close.

Joshua 4:7 Then ye shall answer them, That the waters of Jordan were cut off before the ark of the covenant of the LORD; when it passed over Jordan, the waters of Jordan were cut off: and these stones shall be for a memorial unto the children of Israel for ever.

Children of the heavenly father safely in his bosom gathers. God is truly the lover of little children, for they are the jewels of the Kingdom, in every one of you. You have been dearly purchased, I speak for myself as well. When the trumpet begins to sound we will all be likened as little children. God is in all through all and above all. And for me, that utterance may be given unto me, that I may open my mouth boldly, to make known a living testimony to the mystery of the Gospel.

For which I am an ambassador in bonds: that therein I may speak boldly, as I ought to speak.

There is nothing more precious than mankind realizing the golden gates and the opening of a new era and a new time where we can come United and live out the true meaning of our Creed and the endowed belief of who we are, with the pressing labor in that God we trust, that we would become servants one to another, from whom doctrine of sacrifice reveals.

When the trumpet speaks it will reveal God's original intent and give Mercy and comfort and consolations of peace to mankind and elect nation. Doesn't it say in the Christmas hymn beautiful savior king of creation Jesus shines brighter Jesus shines Purer. Or the Christmas hymn pahrumpa pum pum I am a poor boy too I certainly feel this in myself I do not hold myself that I'm better in some way or another but I am flesh and blood, with the holiness of obedience. God is Divine and is part of a spectrum or rainbow of interpretations and is revealed based on ones own experience and soul condition.

The capital sin of mankind is ignorance, I do not like ignorance at all it gives you a clean slate while other people suffer. Ignorance can be found in many different personalities. If there would be one sin to hate that would be it ignorance has caused so much problems in this world we don't need it in the world to come we need diligence we need curiosity we need patience, we need peculiar personalities we need intrigued we need people that are open thinkers people that support something even if it is a visionary interpretation.

Voice of the centennials is probably my favorite.

(Voice of the centennials) crying out loud there on Mount Zion
the trumpets do dwell Holy Jerusalem oh what a glow,

That fruitful harbor our high aim, Around the world come
yield to the Father's Mercy "Give me your tired, your poor,
your huddled masses yearning to breathe free" come into the
New Jerusalem the city of a living God, the declaration of new
Liberties.

Children suffering around the world starved homeless people,
people that don't have a refuge. Many battered with violence
and war, we have neglected humanity. I honestly have admit
we are all walking through the valley of the shadow death or
the night darkest before the dawn, what I mean is that there
should never be a separation of government rather should be
one ruling Government helping those that are in need across
the world. Oftentimes we have a natural tendency to look the
other way and not help people that are in need. How does it go
for your experience do you see how neglected we have been to
neighboring countries around the world, yeah we don't have to
go far even looking or meeting our neighbor in the right way.

Isaiah 9:6 For unto us a child is born, unto us a son is given:
and the government shall be upon his shoulder: and his name

shall be called Wonderful, Counsellor, The mighty God, The everlasting Father, The Prince of Peace.

1 Thessalonians 4:16 For the Lord himself shall descend from heaven with a shout, with the voice of the archangel, and with the trump of God:

What is depicted here is understood by the nature of God, He is a God of Order. This is referred to as a shout from the descended heavens and this truly must be something that is loud and undeniably true that's the shout we're talking about. Ecstatic energies across cities around the world something new is coming, something new is coming, something new is coming, something new is coming, this is the biggest party on Earth with biblical proportions more that this earth has ever seen or witnessed it's almost like watching something that defies the laws of physics in awe. As President of the United States of America as a due process and to the manner of respect in God we trust, the United States of America has an excellent platform for the Deliverance of the Son of man or Spiritual Jesus.

My Brand name Nova Goshen which is another name as of Saint John.

John 1:26-27 John answered them, saying, I baptize with water: but there standeth one among you, (whom ye know not)

He it is, who coming after me is preferred before me, whose shoe's latchet I am not worthy to unloose

I'm 46 years old I've been carrying this silent ambition since I was a young boy I've been through a lot in my life, there stands one among us, whom you know not. That's why I'm writing this book about Prince of Peace it's the only way I can fully most exhaust everything that I have inside me and to what is revealed at the moment. I don't see myself as a prophet I only see myself as laborer in the Lord's vineyard, Spiritual Jesus, if there would be one name I would like to be it would be the name of Jesus so if people are saluting me or saying hi to me I really feel like the name Jesus has such a bridal effect it bonds to the core of my belief.

Hebrews 12:24 And to Jesus the mediator of the new covenant, and to the blood of sprinkling, that speaketh better things than that of Abel. For our God is a consuming fire. He shall baptize with fire and the Holy Ghost and the removing of those not shaken, not earth alone but heaven also, for I come to bring fire on the Earth, (what would I if it be already kindled).

For God is The Good Shepherd of our soul and we turn to him in prayer and long suffering that we endure all things in the presence of Holy Angels we are One and unite together bearing one another's burdens.

Softly and tenderly Jesus is calling, calling for you and for me, we are working together and we are also shepherds one of another. God's eternal flame he'll never leave nor forsake. That the body is so fitly going together. For He is the head of the body and is the head of the church to one fold in Christ.

Revelation 3:10-11 Because thou hast kept the word of my patience, I also will keep thee from the hour of temptation, which shall come upon all the world, to try them that dwell upon the earth.

Behold, I come quickly: hold that fast which thou hast, that no man take thy crown.

Certainly have kept the word in patience when the fuel of fire is upon me, I patiently endure.

Ephesians 3:17-18 That Christ may dwell in your hearts by faith; that ye, being rooted and grounded in love,

That in so doing, we may be able to comprehend with (all saints) what is the breadth, and length, and depth, and height;

If we are suffer with the chastisement of God, go thy way patiently and that's what that rooted and grounded in love is about, that nothing shall take the place of eternal God. Rooted in the heart by the door of the Lord Jesus Grounded in the mind by the God's eternal law of righteousness that we pray for strength and wisdom and that God would comfort and strengthen our ways.

The Lord's Prayer

Our Father, who art in heaven,

Hallowed be thy Name,

Thy kingdom come,

Thy will be done,

On earth as it is in heaven.

Give us this day our daily bread.

And forgive us our trespasses,

As we forgive those

Who trespass against us.

And lead us not into temptation,

But deliver us from evil.

For thine is the kingdom,

And the power, and the glory,

For ever and ever.

Amen.

Dear brothers and sisters we are accompanied by so much in this world right now and coldness seems to want to manifest itself all over. The Light of this movement will be bringing Nations together bringing world Peace delivering the substance of Faith, although we have so much differences between us it's like we're all yearning to get something better or our soul is crying.

The day is not long and the Good Shepherd will be standing before us wherever we are there he will be also. The manifestation of Spiritualties is huge ladies and gentlemen we are so fortunate to be at the time that we are in right now, to be seeking nourishment from eternal God.

Lord and Savior to be seeking for someone that has humanity and mankind at the highest level of interest. This is the most important part of my book that that we would bear in mind and understand why it so important that how we treat our neighbors and how we treat one another or how we treat people from around the globe we are losing a battle of darkness that continues to haunt every progress we try to develop and almost seems like there is no hope, that what should I do, these are the questions we ask ourselves.

Jesus name has power eternal, haven't we heard this before in a song that Jesus name will last forever through that name all wrong must flea. Through that name I found salvation, oh is this beautiful do you hear this dear eternal fold, do you hear this dear brothers and sisters of Faith do you understand what it means that you found your salvation, this is amazing we take this as a gift from God something unmerited that's exactly what it is and you know it. (If you can believe it, you can own it) it is simply a gift from God. God will open doors God will open opportunities God will open up his United obedience to the young and his United obedience to the old. Those that suffer across the planet and have lost so much in their life they don't have enough food to support themselves they don't have refuge and families are dispersed. This is what we need to focus on we cannot use our excuses of scholarship or should I say that we have a good job and we don't need to worry about other people no no that's not how we're taught we are human beings we are in a crisis and we need to be compassionate to each other and as the Holy Scripture writes that you would provide yourself a Living sacrifice do you know what a living sacrifices is, oh yes you do. I am not walking on water I'm simply suggesting that we would no longer have the crimes against humanity and that includes the entire elect of God's fold. If I'm able to get a new start well then so should other people be able to get a new start as long as there's life there's Hope and that's the nature we need to go about. I wanted to serve in the church many times I've asked the preachers and none of them wanted to admit that they could simply ask the congregation if it's okay for me to speak today and if it was United with the congregation that that would be so then I would be able to preach but they were not able to do that in particular alone. The stone which the builders rejected or disallowed will become the Chief cornerstone disallowed by men but chosen of God and precious. I was chosen of God through revelation. I am like a prodigal son or a black sheep I have a rebel side although yes I like my peace I'm not rich I'm simply a Lyft driver and independent I haven't had a relationship in over 6 years. I always admired modesty and I found a girl in Stockholm that is a model and I never left my faith, hoping someday we would be able to be together I don't even know her name but it's something that I felt was sacred to honor a girl that has modesty and she is definitely very cute. In one of her pictures she's wearing a black watch and it says that she is listening to her biological clock.

Revelation 14:14-15 And I looked, and behold a white cloud, and upon the cloud one sat like unto the Son of man, having on his head a golden crown, and in his hand a sharp sickle.

And another angel came out of the temple, crying with a loud voice to him that sat on the cloud, Thrust in thy sickle, and reap: for the time Is come for thee to reap; for the harvest of the earth is ripe.

That white cloud is the comforter that's what we're waiting for those that shall mourn shall be comforted, I do have a sharp sickle what that means is I have the cognitive ability to perceive and develop food for thought and also explain in detail sophisticated apparatuses whether it's product development or philosophy or spirituality. To beware my pruning hooks are Sharp when it comes to God's righteousness it is with love that reminds us of our weaknesses.

The trumpet sounding on its arrival is yes definitely, A Loud Voice, God's loud singing voice will awaken your hearts. Just as if a little boy for the first time got to actually open his Christmas gift and exposing the innocent within, do you see this child, can you cradle this child in your heart, this is truly The child we're talking about. Jesus said that he put him in the midst of them. Right now I am only in the midst of you.

And Jesus called a little child unto him, and set him in the midst of them.

This next segment God anchored my soul with this revelation when I read it there was no doubt that God will be with me. This happened probably close to 20 years ago

Revelation 2: To him that overcometh will I give to eat of the hidden manna, and will give him a white stone, and in the stone a new name written, which no man knoweth saving he that receiveth it.

Prince of Peace book and what is revealing now is the hidden manna that I was gathering and the white stone is the Holy Ghost. There are so many different spiritual patterns that can be interpreted in so many different ways it's just amazing how intricate but also the spectrum of spirituality.

Psalms 118:4-5 Let them now that fear the LORD say, that his mercy endureth for ever.

I called upon the LORD in distress: the LORD answered me, and set me in a large place.

Spacious glowing and awe, heavenly Host singing hallelujah.

Luke 12:34 For where your treasure is, there will your heart be also.

For if you then be risen with Christ seek those things which are above.

Alpha and Omega Son of the Living God, Jesus Redeemer Prince of Peace, for the drawing of Redemption and the Reconciliation of God.

Revelation 3:8 I know thy works: behold, I have set before thee an open door, and no man can shut it: for thou hast a little strength, and hast kept my word, and hast not denied my name.

Jesus,

1 Corinthians 9:24 Know ye not that they which run in a race run all, but one receiveth the prize? So run, that ye may obtain.

I will be bringing the kingdom of heaven, the Kingdom of heaven is like hopping in a cocoon and coming out feeling like a butterfly. I designed conceptual development is the three dimensional augmented virtual reality you can actually go into the cocoon and sit next to a tree and watch the Snow White and the seven dwarfs. This is an experience that exceeds what you would see in the natural reality. The kingdom of heaven is a supernatural encounter. Everything is perfect with High Definition, consuming with awe.

If you want to fund or support me in efforts to Presidency, be free to contact me on Facebook John Nels Ruonavaara or

Cash app

$JohnRuonavaara3

www.ingramcontent.com/pod-product-compliance
Lightning Source LLC
Chambersburg PA
CBHW060356130626
46553CB00003B/1258